Iphigenia In Aulis by Euripides

Euripides is rightly lauded as one of the great dramatists of all time. In his lifetime, he wrote over 90 plays and although only 18 have survived they reveal the scope and reach of his genius.

Euripides is identified with many theatrical innovations that have influenced drama all the way down to modern times, especially in the representation of traditional, mythical heroes as ordinary people in extraordinary circumstances.

As would be expected from a life lived 2,500 years ago, details of it are few and far between. Accounts of his life, written down the ages, do exist but whether much is reliable or surmised is open to debate.

Most accounts agree that he was born on Salamis Island around 480 BC, to mother Cleito and father Mnesarchus, a retailer who lived in a village near Athens. Upon the receipt of an oracle saying that his son was fated to win "crowns of victory", Mnesarchus insisted that the boy should train for a career in athletics.

However, what is clear is that athletics was not to be the way to win crowns of victory. Euripides had been lucky enough to have been born in the era as the other two masters of Greek Tragedy; Sophocles and Æschylus. It was in their footsteps that he was destined to follow.

His first play was performed some thirteen years after the first of Socrates plays and a mere three years after Æschylus had written his classic The Oristria.

Theatre was becoming a very important part of the Greek culture. The Dionysia, held annually, was the most important festival of theatre and second only to the fore-runner of the Olympic games, the Panathenia, held every four years, in appeal.

Euripides first competed in the City Dionysia, in 455 BC, one year after the death of Æschylus, and, incredibly, it was not until 441 BC that he won first prize. His final competition in Athens was in 408 BC. The Bacchae and Iphigenia in Aulis were performed after his death in 405 BC and first prize was awarded posthumously. Altogether his plays won first prize only five times.

Euripides was also a great lyric poet. In Medea, for example, he composed for his city, Athens, "the noblest of her songs of praise". His lyric skills however are not just confined to individual poems: "A play of Euripides is a musical whole....one song echoes motifs from the preceding song, while introducing new ones."

Much of his life and his whole career coincided with the struggle between Athens and Sparta for hegemony in Greece but he didn't live to see the final defeat of his city.

Euripides fell out of favour with his fellow Athenian citizens and retired to the court of Archelaus, king of Macedon, who treated him with consideration and affection.

At his death, in around 406BC, he was mourned by the king, who, refusing the request of the Athenians that his remains be carried back to the Greek city, buried him with much splendor within his own dominions. His tomb was placed at the confluence of two streams, near Arethusa in Macedonia, and a cenotaph was built to his memory on the road from Athens towards the Piraeus.

Index of Contents

THE PERSONS

AGAMEMNON.
OLD MAN.
MENELAUS.
ACHILLES.
MESSENGER.
ANOTHER MESSENGER.
IPHIGENIA.
CLYTÆMNESTRA.
CHORUS.

THE ARGUMENT

When the Greeks were detained at Aulis by stress of weather, Calchas declared that they would never reach Troy unless the daughter of Agamemnon, Iphigenia, was sacrificed to Diana. Agamemnon sent for his daughter with this view, but repenting, he dispatched a messenger to prevent Clytæmnestra sending her. The messenger being intercepted by Menelaus, an altercation between the brother chieftains arose, during which Iphigenia, who had been tempted with the expectation of being wedded to Achilles, arrived with her mother. The latter, meeting with Achilles, discovered the deception, and Achilles swore to protect her. But Iphigenia, having determined to die nobly on behalf of the Greeks, was snatched away by the Goddess, and a stag substituted in her place. The Greeks were then enabled to set sail.

IPHIGENIA IN AULIS

AGAMEMNON, OLD MAN

AGAMEMNON
Come before this dwelling, O aged man.

OLD MAN
I come. But what new thing dost thou meditate, king Agamemnon?

AGAMEMNON
You shall learn.

OLD MAN
I hasten. My old age is very sleepless, and sits wakeful upon mine eyes.

AGAMEMNON

What star can this be that traverses this way?

OLD MAN

Sirius, flitting yet midway between the heavens and the ocean, close to the seven Pleiads.

AGAMEMNON

No longer therefore is there the sound either of birds or of the sea, but silence of the winds reigns about this Euripus.

OLD MAN

But why art thou hastening without the tent, king Agamemnon? But still there is silence here by Aulis, and the guards of the fortifications are undisturbed. Let us go within.

AGAMEMNON

I envy thee, old man, and I envy that man who has passed through a life without danger, unknown, unglorious; but I less envy those in honor.

OLD MAN

And yet 'tis in this that the glory of life is.

AGAMEMNON

But this very glory is uncertain, for the love of popularity is pleasant indeed, but hurts when present. Sometimes the worship of the Gods not rightly conducted upturns one's life, and sometimes the many and dissatisfied opinions of men harass.

OLD MAN

I praise not these remarks in a chieftain. O Agamemnon, Atreus did not beget thee upon a condition of complete good fortune. But thou needs must rejoice and grieve; in turn, for thou art a mortal born, and even though you wish it not, the will of the Gods will be thus. But thou, opening the light of a lamp, art both writing this letter, which thou still art carrying in thy hands, and again you blot out the same characters, and seal, and loose again, and cast the tablet to the ground, pouring abundant tears, and thou lackest naught of the unwonted things that tend to madness. Why art thou troubled, why art thou troubled? What new thing, what new thing has happened concerning thee, O king? Come, communicate discourse with me. But thou wilt speak to a good and faithful man, for to thy wife Tyndarus sent me once on a time, as a dower-gift, and disinterested companion.

AGAMEMNON

To Leda, daughter of Thestias, were born three virgins, Phœbe, and Clytæmnestra my spouse, and Helen. Of this latter, the youths of Greece that were in the first state of prosperity came as suitors. But terrible threats of bloodshed arose against one another, from whoever should not obtain the virgin. But the matter was difficult for her father Tyndarus, whether to give, or not to give her in marriage, and how he might best deal with the circumstances, when this occurred to him; that the suitors should join oaths and plight right hands with one another, and over burnt-offerings should enter into treaty, and bind themselves by this oath, "Of whomsoever the daughter of Tyndarus shall become wife, that they will join to assist him, if any one should depart from his house taking her with him, and excluding the possessor from his bed, and that they will make an expedition in arms, and sack the city of the ravisher, Greek or barbarian alike." But after they had pledged themselves, the old man Tyndarus somehow cleverly overreached them by a cunning plan. He permits his daughter to choose one of the suitors, toward whom the friendly gales of Venus might impel her.

But she chose (whom would she had never taken!) Menelaus. And he who, according to the story told by men, once judged the Goddesses, coming from Phrygia to Lacedæmon, flowered in the vesture of his garments, and glittering with gold, barbarian finery, loving Helen who loved him, he stole and bore her away to the bull-stalls of Ida, having found Menelaus abroad. But he, goaded hastily through Greece, calls to witness the old oath given to Tyndarus, that it behooves to assist the aggrieved. Henceforth the Greeks hastening with the spear, having taken their arms, come to this Aulis with its narrow straits, with ships and shields together, and accoutred with many horses and chariots. And they chose me general of the host, out of regard for Menelaus, being his brother forsooth. And would that some other than I had obtained the dignity. But when the army was assembled and levied, we sat, having no power of sailing, at Aulis. But Calchas the seer proclaimed to us, being at a loss, that we should sacrifice Iphigenia, whom I begat, to Diana, who inhabits this place, and that if we sacrificed her, we should have both our voyage, and the sacking of Troy, but that this should not befall us if we did not sacrifice her. But I hearing this in rousing proclamation, bade Talthybius dismiss the whole army, as I should never have the heart to slay my daughter. Upon this, indeed, my brother, alleging every kind of reasoning, persuaded me to dare the dreadful deed, and having written in the folds of a letter, I sent word to my wife to send her daughter as if to be married to Achilles, both enlarging on the dignity of the man, and asserting that he would not sail with the Greeks, unless a wife for him from among us should come to Phthia. For I had this means of persuading my wife, having made up a pretended match for the virgin. But we alone of the Greeks know how these matters are, Calchas, Ulysses, and Nestor. But the things which I then determined not well, I am now differently writing so as to be well, in this letter, which by the shadow of night thou beheldest me opening and closing, old man. But come, go thou, taking these letters, to Argos. But as to what the letter conceals in its folds, I will tell thee in words all that is written therein; for thou art faithful to my wife and house.

OLD MAN
Speak, and tell me, that with my tongue I may also say what agrees with your letter.

AGAMEMNON [Reading]
"I send to thee, O germ of Leda, besides my former dispatches, not to send thy daughter to the bay-like wing of Eubœa, waveless Aulis. For we will delay the bridals of our daughter till another season."

OLD MAN
And how will not Achilles raise up his temper against thee and thy wife, showing great wrath at failing of his spouse? This also is terrible. Show what thou meanest.

AGAMEMNON
Achilles, furnishing the pretext, not the reality, knows not these nuptials, nor what we are doing; nor that I have professed to give my daughter into the nuptial chain of his arms by marriage.

OLD MAN
Thou venturest terrible things, king Agamemnon, who, having promised thy daughter as wife to the son of the Goddess, dost lead her as a sacrifice on behalf of the Greeks.

AGAMEMNON
Ah me! I was out of my senses. Alas! And I am falling into calamity. But go, plying thy foot, yielding naught to old age.

OLD MAN
I hasten, O king.

AGAMEMNON

Do not thou either sit down by the woody fountains, nor repose in sleep.

OLD MAN

Speak good words.

AGAMEMNON

But every where as you pass the double track, look about, watching lest there escape thee a chariot passing with swift wheels, bearing my daughter hither to the ships of the Greeks.

OLD MAN

This shall be.

AGAMEMNON

And go out of the gates quickly, for if you meet with the procession, again go forth, shake the reins, going to the temples reared by the Cyclops.

OLD MAN

But tell me, how, saying this, I shall obtain belief from thy daughter and wife.

AGAMEMNON

Preserve the seal, this which thou bearest on this letter. Go: morn, already dawning forth this light, grows white, and the fire of the sun's four steeds. Aid me in my toils. But no one of mortals is prosperous or blest to the last, for none hath yet been born free from pain.

CHORUS

I came to the sands of the shore of marine Aulis, having sailed through the waves of Euripus, quitting Chalcis with its narrow strait, my city, the nurse of the sea-neighboring waters of renowned Arethusa, in order that I might behold the army of the Greeks, and the ship-conveying oars of the Grecian youths, whom against Troy in a thousand ships of fir, our husbands say that yellow-haired Menelaus and Agamemnon of noble birth, are leading in quest of Helen, whom the herdsman Paris bore from reed-nourishing Eurotas, a gift of Venus, when at the fountain dews Venus held contest, contest respecting beauty with Juno and Pallas. But I came swiftly through the wood of Diana with its many sacrifices, making my cheek red with youthful modesty, wishing to behold the defense of the shield, and the arm-bearing tents of the Greeks, and the crowd of steeds. But I saw the two Ajaces companions, the son of Oileus, and the son of Telamon, the glory of Salamis, and Protesilaus and Palamedes, whom the daughter of Neptune bore, diverting themselves with the complicated figures of draughts, and Diomede rejoicing in the pleasures of the disk, and by them Merione, the blossom of Mars, a marvel to mortals, and the son of Laertes from the mountains of the isle, and with them Nireus, fairest of the Greeks, and Achilles, tempest-like in the course, fleet as the winds, whom Thetis bore, and Chiron trained up, I beheld him on the shore, coursing in arms along the shingles. And he toiled through a contest of feet, running against a chariot of four steeds for victory. But the charioteer cried out, Eumelus, the grandson of Pheres, whose most beauteous steeds I beheld, decked out with gold-tricked bits, hurried on by the lash, the middle ones in yoke dappled with white-spotted hair, but those outside, in loose harness, running contrariwise in the bendings of the course, bays, with dappled skins under their legs with solid hoofs. Close by which Pelides was running in arms, by the orb and wheels of the chariot. And I came to the multitude of ships, a sight not to be described, that I might satiate the sight of my woman's eyes, a sweet delight. And at the right horn of the fleet was the Phthiotic army of the Myrmidons, with fifty valiant ships. And in golden effigies the Nereid Goddesses stood on the summit of the poops, the standard of the host of

Achilles. And next to these there stood the Argive ships, with equal number of oars, of which Euryalus the grandson of Mecisteus was general, whom his father Talaus trains up, and Sthenelus son of Capaneus. But Acamas son of Theseus, leading sixty ships from Athens, kept station, having the Goddess Pallas placed in her equestrian winged chariot, a prosperous sign to sailors. But I beheld the armament of the Bœotians, fifty sea-bound ships, with signs at the figure-heads, and their sign was Cadmus, holding a golden dragon, at the beaks of the ships, and Leitus the earth-born was leader of the naval armament, and I beheld those from the Phocian land. But the son of Oileus, leading an equal number of Locrian ships, came, having left the Thronian city. But from Cyclopian Mycenæ the son of Atreus sent the assembled mariners of a hundred ships. And with him was Adrastus, as friend with friend, in order that Greece might wreak vengeance on those who fled their homes, for the sake of barbarian nuptials. But from Pylos we beheld on the poops of Gerenian Nestor, a sign bull-footed to view, his neighbor Alpheus. But there were twelve beaks of Ænian ships, which king Gyneus led, and near these again the chieftains of Elis, whom all the people named Epeians, and o'er these Eurytus had power. But the white-oared Taphian host (*) led, which Meges ruled, the offspring of Phyleus, leaving the island Echinades, inaccessible to sailors. And Ajax, the foster-child of Salamis, joined the right horn to the left, to which he was stationed nearest, joining them with his furthermost ships, with twelve most swift vessels, as I heard, and beheld the naval people. To which if any one add the barbarian barks, it will not obtain a return. Where I beheld the naval expedition, but hearing other things at home I preserve remembrance of the assembled army.

(*) *there are several words missing here.*

OLD MAN
Menelaus, thou art daring dreadful deeds thou shouldst not dare.

MENELAUS
Away with thee! thou art too faithful to thy masters.

OLD MAN
An honorable rebuke thou hast rebuked me with!

MENELAUS
To thy cost shall it be, if thou dost that thou shouldst not do.

OLD MAN
You have no right to open the letter which I was carrying.

MENELAUS
Nor shouldst thou bear ills to all the Greeks.

OLD MAN
Contest this point with others, but give up this letter to me.

MENELAUS
I will not let it go.

OLD MAN
Nor will I let it go.

MENELAUS
Then quickly with my sceptre will I make thine head bloody.

OLD MAN

But glorious it is to die for one's masters.

MENELAUS

Let go. Being a slave, thou speakest too many words.

OLD MAN

O master, I am wronged, and this man, having snatched thy letter out of my hands, O Agamemnon, is unwilling to act rightly.

MENELAUS

Ah! what is this tumult and disorder of words?

OLD MAN

My words, not his, are fittest to speak.

AGAMEMNON

But wherefore, Menelaus, dost thou come to strife with this man and art dragging him by force?

MENELAUS

Look at me, that I may take this commencement of my speech.

AGAMEMNON

What, shall I through fear not open mine eyelids, being born of Atreus?

MENELAUS

Seest thou this letter, the minister of writings most vile?

AGAMEMNON

I see it, and do thou first let it go from thy hands.

MENELAUS

Not, at least, before I show to the Greeks what is written therein.

AGAMEMNON

What, knowest thou what 'tis unseasonable thou shouldst know, having broken the seal?

MENELAUS

Ay, so as to pain thee, having unfolded the ills thou hast wrought privily.

AGAMEMNON

But where didst thou obtain it? O Gods, for thy shameless heart!

MENELAUS

Expecting thy daughter from Argos, whether she will come to the army.

AGAMEMNON

What behooves thee to keep watch upon my affairs? Is not this the act of a shameless man?

MENELAUS

Because the will to do so teased me, and I am not born thy slave.

AGAMEMNON
Is it not dreadful? Shall I not be suffered to be master of my own family?

MENELAUS
For thou thinkest inconsistently, now one thing, before another, another thing presently.

AGAMEMNON
Well hast thou talked evil. Hateful is a too clever tongue.

MENELAUS
But an unstable mind is an unjust thing to possess, and not clear for friends. I wish to expostulate with thee, but do not thou in wrath turn away from the truth, nor will I speak overlong. Thou knowest when thou wast making interest to be leader of the Greeks against Troy—in seeming indeed not wishing it, but wishing it in will—how humble thou wast, taking hold of every right hand, and keeping open doors to any of the people that wished, and giving audience to all in turn even if one wished it not, seeking by manners to purchase popularity among the multitude. But when you obtained the power, changing to different manners, you were no longer the same friend as before to your old friends, difficult of access, and rarely within doors. But it behooves not a man who has met with great fortune to change his manners, but then chiefly to be firm toward his friends, when he is best able to benefit them, being prosperous. I have first gone over these charges against thee, in which I first found thee base. But when thou afterward camest into Aulis and to the army of all the Greeks, thou wast naught, but wast in stupefaction at the fortune which then befell us from the Gods, lacking a favorable breeze for the journey. But the Greeks demanded that you should dismiss the ships, and not toil vainly at Aulis. But how cheerless and distressed a countenance you wore, because you were not able to land your army at Priam's land, having a thousand ships under command. And thou besoughtest me, "What shall I do?" "But what resource shall I find from whence?" so that thou mightest not lose an ill renown, being deprived of the command. And then, when Calchas o'er the victims said that thou must sacrifice thy daughter to Diana, and that there would then be means of sailing for the Greeks, delighted in heart, you gladly promised to sacrifice your child, and of your own accord, not by compulsion—do not say so—you send to your wife to convoy your daughter hither, on a pretext of being wedded to Achilles. And then changing your mind you are caught altering to other writings, to the effect that you will not now be the slayer of your daughter. Very pretty, forsooth! This is the same air which heard these very protestations from thee. But innumerable men experience this in their affairs; they persevere in labor when in power, and then make a bad result, sometimes through the foolish mind of the citizens, but sometimes with reason, themselves becoming incapable of preserving the state, I indeed chiefly groan for hapless Greece, who, wishing to work some doughty deed against these good-for-nothing barbarians, will let them, laughing at us, slip through her hands, on account of thee and thy daughter. I would not make any one ruler of the land for the sake of necessity, nor chieftain of armed men. It behooves the general of the state to possess sense, for every man is a ruler who possesses sense.

CHORUS
'Tis dreadful for words and strife to happen between brothers, when they fall into dispute.

AGAMEMNON
I wish to address thee in evil terms, but mildly, in brief, not uplifting mine eyelids too much aloft through insolence, but moderately, as being my brother. For a good man is wont to show respect to others. Tell me, why dost thou burst forth thus violently, having thy face suffused with rage? Who wrongs thee? What lackest thou? Wouldst fain gain a good wife! I can not supply thee, for thou didst

ill rule over the one you possessed. Must I therefore pay the penalty of your mismanagement, who have made no mistake? Or does my ambition annoy thee? But wouldst thou fain hold in thine arms a fair woman, forgetting discretion and honor? Evil pleasures belong to an evil man. But if I, having before resolved ill, have changed to good counsel, am I mad? Rather art thou mad, who, having lost a bad wife, desirest to recover her, when God has well prospered thy fortune. The nuptial-craving suitors in their folly swore the oath to Tyndarus, but hope, I ween, was their God, and wrought this more than thyself and thy strength. Whom taking make thou the expedition, but I think thou wilt know that it is through the folly of their hearts, for the divinity is not ignorant, but is capable of discerning oaths ill plighted and perforce. But I will not slay my children, so that thy state will in justice be well, revenge upon the worst of wives, but nights and days will waste me away in tears, having wrought lawless, unjust deeds against the children whom I begat. These words are briefly spoken to thee, both plain and easy, but if thou art unwilling to be wise, I will arrange my own affairs well.

CHORUS
These words are different from those before spoken, but they are to a good effect, that the children be spared.

MENELAUS
Alas! alas! have I then wretched no friends?

AGAMEMNON
Yes, you have, at least, if you do not wish to ruin your friends.

MENELAUS
But how will you show that you are born of the same sire with me?

AGAMEMNON
I am born to be wise with you, not foolish.

MENELAUS
It behooves friends to grieve in common with friends.

AGAMEMNON
Admonish me by well doing, not by paining me.

MENELAUS
Dost thou not then think fit to toil through this with Greece?

AGAMEMNON
But Greece, with thee, is sickening through some deity.

MENELAUS
Vaunt then on thy sceptre, having betrayed thy brother. But I will seek some other schemes, and other friends.

[Enter a **MESSENGER**.

MESSENGER
O Agamemnon, king of all the Greeks, I am come, bringing thy daughter to thee, whom thou didst name Iphigenia in thy palace. But her mother follows, the person of thy wife Clytæmnestra, and the

boy Orestes, that thou mayest be pleased at the sight, being away from thine home a long season. But as they have come a long way, they and their mares are refreshing their female feet by the fair-flowing fountain, and we let loose the mares in a grassy meadow, that they might taste fodder. But I am come before them to prepare you for their reception, for a swift report passed through the army, that thy daughter had arrived. And all the multitude comes out hastily to the spectacle, that they may behold thy child. For prosperous men are renowned and conspicuous among all mortals. And they say, "Is there a marriage on foot? or what is going on?" Or, "Has king Agamemnon, having a yearning after his daughter, brought his child hither?" But from some you would have heard this: "They are initiating the damsel in honor of Artemis, queen of Aulis, who will marry her." But come, get ready the baskets, which come next, crown thine head. And do thou, king Menelaus, prepare a nuptial lay, and through the house let the pipe sound and let there be noise of feet, for this day comes blessed upon the virgin.

AGAMEMNON
I commend your words, but go thou within the house, and it shall be well, as fortune takes its course. Alas! what shall I wretched say? Whence shall I begin? Into what fetters of necessity have I fallen! Fortune has upturned me, so as to become far too clever for my cleverness. But lowness of birth has some advantage thus. For such persons are at liberty to weep, and speak unhappy words, but to him that is of noble birth, all these things belong. We have our dignity as ruler of our life, and are slaves to the multitude. For I am ashamed indeed to let fall the tear, yet again wretched am I ashamed not to weep, having come into the greatest calamities. Well! what shall I say to my wife? How shall I receive her? What manner of countenance shall I present? And truly she hath undone me, coming uncalled amidst the ills which before possessed me. And with reason did she follow her daughter, being about to deck her as a bride, and to perform the dearest offices, where she will find us base. But for this hapless virgin—why call her virgin? Hades, as it seems, will speedily attend on her nuptials,—how do I pity her! For I think that she will beseech me thus: O father, wilt thou slay me? Such a wedding mayest thou thyself wed, and whosoever is a friend to thee. But Orestes being present will cry out knowingly words not knowing, for he is yet an infant. Alas! how has Priam's son, Paris, undone me by wedding the nuptials of Paris, who has wrought this!

CHORUS
And I also pity her, as it becomes a stranger woman to moan for the misfortune of her lords.

MENELAUS
Brother, give me thy right hand to touch.

AGAMEMNON
I give it, for thine is the power, but I am wretched.

MENELAUS
I swear by Pelops, who was called the sire of my father and thine, and my father Atreus, that I indeed will tell thee plainly from my heart, and not any thing out of contrivance, but only what I think. I, beholding thee letting fall the tear from thine eyes, pitied thee, and myself let fall a tear for thee in return. And I have changed my old determinations, not being wrath against you, but I will place myself in your present situation, and I recommend you neither to slay your child, nor to take my part; for it is not just that thou shouldst groan, but my affairs be in a pleasant state, and that thine should die, but mine behold the light. For what do I wish? Might I not obtain another choice alliance, if I crave nuptials? But, having undone my brother, whom it least behooved me, shall I receive Helen, an evil in place of a good? I was foolish and young, before that, viewing the matter closely, I saw what it is to beget children. Besides, pity came over me, considering our connection, for the hapless girl, who is about to be sacrificed because of my marriage. But what has thy virgin

daughter to do with Helen? Let the army go, being disbanded from Aulis. But cease thou bedewing thine eyes with tears, my brother, and exciting me to tears. But if I have any concern in the oracle respecting thy daughter, let me have none: to thee I yield my part. But I have come to a change from terrible resolutions. I have experienced what was meet. I have changed to regard him who is sprung from a common source. Such changes belong not to a bad man, to follow the best always.

CHORUS
Thou hast spoken generous words, and becoming Tantalus the son of Jove. Thou disgracest not thine ancestors.

AGAMEMNON
I commend thee, Menelaus, in that, contrary to my expectation, you have subjoined these words, rightly, and worthily of thee.

MENELAUS
A certain disturbance between brothers arises on account of love, and avarice in their houses. I abhor such a relationship, mutually sore.

AGAMEMNON
But consider, for we are come into circumstances that render it necessary to accomplish the bloody slaughter of my daughter.

MENELAUS
How? Who will compel thee to slay thy child?

AGAMEMNON
The whole assembly of the armament of the Greeks.

MENELAUS
Not so, if at least thou dismiss it back to Argos.

AGAMEMNON
In this matter I might escape discovery, but in that I can not.

MENELAUS
What? One should not too much fear the multitude.

AGAMEMNON
Calchas will proclaim his prophecy to the army of the Greeks.

MENELAUS
Not if he die first—and this is easy.

AGAMEMNON
The whole race of seers is an ambitious ill.

MENELAUS
And in naught good or profitable, when at hand.

AGAMEMNON
But dost thou not fear that which occurs to me?

MENELAUS

How can I understand the word you say not?

AGAMEMNON

The son of Sisyphus knows all these matters.

MENELAUS

It can not be that Orestes can pain thee and me.

AGAMEMNON

He is ever changeable, and with the multitude.

MENELAUS

He is indeed possessed with the passion for popularity, a dreadful evil.

AGAMEMNON

Do you not then think that he, standing in the midst of the Greeks, will tell the oracles which Calchas pronounced, and of me, that I promised to offer a sacrifice to Diana, and then break my word. With which words having carried away the army, he will bid the Greeks slay thee and me, and sacrifice the damsel. And if I flee to Argos, they will come and ravage and raze the land, Cyclopean walls and all. Such are my troubles. O unhappy me! How, by the Gods, am I at a loss in these present matters! Take care of one thing for me, Menelaus, going through the army, that Clytæmnestra may not learn these matters, before I take and offer my daughter to Hades, that I may fare ill with as few tears as possible. But do ye, O stranger women, preserve silence.

CHORUS

Blest are they who share the nuptial bed of the Goddess Aphrodite, when she is moderate, and with modesty, obtaining a calm from the maddening stings, when Love with his golden locks stretches his twin bow of graces, the one for a prosperous fate, the other for the upturning of life. I deprecate this bow, O fairest Venus, from our beds, but may mine be a moderate grace, and holy endearments, and may I share Aphrodite, but reject her when excessive. But the natures of mortals are different, and their manners are different, but that which is clearly good is ever plain. And the education which trains men up, conduces greatly to virtue, for to have reverence is wisdom, and it possesses an equivalent advantage, viz. to perceive what is fitting by one's mind, where report bears unwasting glory to life. 'Tis a great thing to hunt for the praise of virtue, among women indeed, by a secret affection, but among men, on the other hand, honor being inherent, bears that praise, honor, which increases a state to an incalculable extent.

Thou earnest, O Paris, where thou wast trained up a shepherd with the white heifers of Ida, trilling a barbarian lay, breathing an imitation of the Phrygian pipes of Olympus on a reed. And the cows with their well-filled udders browsed, when the judgment of the Goddesses drove thee mad, which sends thee into Greece, before the ivory-decked palaces, thou who didst strike love into the eyes of Helen which were upon thee, and thyself wast fluttered with love. Whence strife, strife brings Greece against the bulwarks of Troy with spears and ships. Alas! alas! great are the fortunes of the great. Behold the king's daughter, Iphigenia, my queen, and Clytæmnestra, daughter of Tyndarus, how are they sprung from the great, and to what suitable fortune they are come. The powerful, in sooth, and the wealthy, are Gods to those of mortals who are unblest. Let us stand still, ye children of Chalcis, let us receive the queen from her chariot to the earth, not unsteadily, but gently with the soft attention of our hands, lest the renowned daughter of Agamemnon, newly coming to me, be alarmed, nor let us, as strangers to strangers, cause disturbance or fear to the Argive ladies.

[Enter **CLYTÆMNESTRA, IPHIGENIA**, and **ORESTES** in a chariot. They descend from it, while the **CHORUS** make obeisance.

CLYTÆMNESTRA
I regard both your kindness and your favorable words as a good omen, and I have some hope that I am here as escort of my daughter to honorable nuptials. But take out of my chariot the dower-gifts which I bear for my girl, and send them carefully into the house. And do thou, my child, quit the horse-chariot, setting carefully thy foot delicate and at the same time tender. But you, maidens, receive her in your arms, and lift her from the chariot. And let some one give me the firm support of his hand, that I may beseemingly leave the chariot-seat. But do some of you stand in front of the horses' yoke, for the uncontrolled eye of horses is timorous, and take this boy, the son of Agamemnon, Orestes, for he is still an infant. Child! dost sleep, overcome by the ride? Wake up happily for thy sisters' nuptials. For thou thyself being noble shalt obtain relationship with a good man, the God-like son of the daughter of Nereus. Next come thou close to my foot, O daughter, to thy mother, Iphigenia, and standing near, show these strangers how happy I am, and come hither indeed, and address thy dear father. O thou most great glory to me, king Agamemnon, we are come, not disobeying thy bidding.

IPHIGENIA
O mother, running indeed, but be thou not angry, I will apply my breast to my father's breast. But I wish, rushing to embrace thy breast, O father, after a long season. For I long for thy face. But do not be angry.

CLYTÆMNESTRA
But, O my child, enjoy thine embraces, but thou wert ever most fond of thy father, of all the children I bore.

IPHIGENIA
O father, joyous do I behold thee after a long season.

AGAMEMNON
And I, thy father, joyously behold thee. Thou speakest thus equally in respect to both.

IPHIGENIA
Hail! But well hast thou done in bringing me to thee, O father.

AGAMEMNON
I know not how I shall say, yet not say so, my child.

IPHIGENIA
Ah! how uneasily dost thou regard me, joyfully beholding me before.

AGAMEMNON
A king and general has many cares.

IPHIGENIA
Give thyself up to me now, and turn not thyself to cares.

AGAMEMNON
But I am altogether concerned with thee, and on no other subject.

IPHIGENIA
Relax thy brow, and open thy eyes in joy.

AGAMEMNON
See, I rejoice as I rejoice, at seeing thee, child.

IPHIGENIA
And then dost let fall a tear from thine eyes?

AGAMEMNON
For long to us is the coming absence.

IPHIGENIA
I know not what you mean, I know not, dearest father mine.

AGAMEMNON
Speaking sensibly, thou movest me the more to pity.

IPHIGENIA
I will speak foolishly, if I so may rejoice you.

AGAMEMNON
Alas! I can not keep silence, but I commend thee.

IPHIGENIA
Remain, O father, in the house with thy children,

AGAMEMNON
I fain would, but not having what I would, I am pained.

IPHIGENIA
Perish war and the ills of Menelaus!

AGAMEMNON
What has undone me will first undo others.

IPHIGENIA
How long a time wast thou absent in the recesses of Aulis!

AGAMEMNON
And now also there is something hinders me from sending on the army.

IPHIGENIA
Where say they that the Phrygians dwell, father?

AGAMEMNON
Where would that Paris, Priam's son, had never dwelt.

IPHIGENIA
And dost thou go a long distance, O father, when thou leavest me?

AGAMEMNON

Thou art come, my daughter, to the same state with thy father.

IPHIGENIA

Alas! would that it were fitting me and thee to take me with thee as thy fellow-sailor.

AGAMEMNON

But there is yet a sailing for thee, where thou wilt remember thy father.

IPHIGENIA

Shall I go, sailing with my mother, or alone?

AGAMEMNON

Alone, apart from thy father and mother.

IPHIGENIA

What, art thou going to make me dwell in other houses, father?

AGAMEMNON

Cease. It is not proper for girls to know these matters.

IPHIGENIA

Hasten back from Phrygia, do, my father, having settled matters well there.

AGAMEMNON

It first behooves me to offer a certain sacrifice here.

IPHIGENIA

But it is with the priests that thou shouldst consider sacred matters.

AGAMEMNON

Yet shalt thou know it, for thou wilt stand round the altar.

IPHIGENIA

What, shall we stand in chorus round the altar, my father?

AGAMEMNON

I deem thee happier than myself, for that thou know-est nothing. But go within the house, that the girls may behold thee, having given me a sad kiss and thy right hand, being about to dwell a long time away from thy sire. O bosom and cheeks, O yellow tresses, how has the city of the Phrygians proved a burden to us, and Helen! I cease my words, for swift does the drop trickle from mine eyes when I touch thee. Go into the house. But I, I crave thy pardon, [To **CLYTÆMNESTRA**] daughter of Leda, if I showed too much feeling, being about to bestow my daughter on Achilles. For the departure of a girl is a happy one, but nevertheless it pains the parents, when a father, who has toiled much, delivers up his children to another home.

CLYTÆMNESTRA

I am not so insensible—but think thou that I shall experience the same feelings, so that I should not chide thee, when I lead forth my girl with nuptial rejoicings, but custom wears away these thoughts in course of time. I know, however, the name of him to whom thou hast promised thy daughter, but I would fain know of what race, and whence he is.

AGAMEMNON
Ægina was the daughter of her father Asopus.

CLYTÆMNESTRA
And who of mortals or of Gods wedded her?

AGAMEMNON
Jove, and she gave birth to Æacus, prince of Œnone.

CLYTÆMNESTRA
But what son obtained the house of Æacus?

AGAMEMNON
Peleus, and Peleus obtained the daughter of Nereus.

CLYTÆMNESTRA
By the gift of the God, or taking her in spite of the Gods?

AGAMEMNON
Jove acted as a sponsor, and bestowed her, having the power.

CLYTÆMNESTRA
And where does he wed her? In the wave of the sea?

AGAMEMNON
Where Chiron dwells at the sacred foot of Pelion.

CLYTÆMNESTRA
Where they say that the race of Centaurs dwells?

AGAMEMNON
Here the Gods celebrated the nuptial feast of Peleus.

CLYTÆMNESTRA
But did Thetis, or his father, train up Achilles?

AGAMEMNON
Chiron, that he might not learn the manners of evil mortals.

CLYTÆMNESTRA
Hah! wise was the instructor, and wiser he who intrusted him.

AGAMEMNON
Such a man will be the husband of thy child.

CLYTÆMNESTRA
Not to be found fault with. But what city in Greece does he inhabit?

AGAMEMNON

Near the river Apidanus in the confines of Phthia.

CLYTÆMNESTRA

Thither will he lead thy virgin daughter and mine.

AGAMEMNON

This shall be the care of him, her possessor.

CLYTÆMNESTRA

And may the pair be happy; but on what day will he wed her?

AGAMEMNON

When the prospering orb of the moon comes round.

CLYTÆMNESTRA

But hast thou already sacrificed the first offerings for thy daughter
to the Goddess?

AGAMEMNON

I am about to do so. In this matter we are now engaged.

CLYTÆMNESTRA

And wilt thou then celebrate a wedding-feast afterward?

AGAMEMNON

Ay, having sacrificed such offerings as it behooves me to sacrifice to the Gods.

CLYTÆMNESTRA

But where shall we set out a banquet for the women?

AGAMEMNON

Here, by the fair-pooped ships of the Greeks.

CLYTÆMNESTRA

Well, and poorly, forsooth! but may it nevertheless turn out well.

AGAMEMNON

Do then thou knowest what, O lady, and obey me.

CLYTÆMNESTRA

In what? for I am accustomed to obey thee.

AGAMEMNON

We indeed in this place, where the bridegroom is—

CLYTÆMNESTRA

Will do what without the mother, of those things which it behoves me to do?

AGAMEMNON

—will bestow your daughter among the Greeks.

CLYTÆMNESTRA
But where must I be in the mean time?

AGAMEMNON
Go to Argos, and take care of your virgins.

CLYTÆMNESTRA
Leaving my child? And who will bear the nuptial torch?

AGAMEMNON
I will furnish the light that becomes the nuptials.

CLYTÆMNESTRA
The custom is not thus, but you think these matters trifles.

AGAMEMNON
It is not proper that thou shouldst mingle in the crowd of the army.

CLYTÆMNESTRA
It is proper that I, the mother, should bestow at least my own daughter.

AGAMEMNON
And it is proper that the damsels at home should not be alone.

CLYTÆMNESTRA
They are well guarded in their close chambers.

AGAMEMNON
Obey me.

CLYTÆMNESTRA
No, by the Argive Goddess queen. But go you, and attend to matters abroad, but I will mind the affairs at home, as to the things which should be present to virgins at their wedding.

AGAMEMNON
Alas! In vain have I toiled, and have been frustrated in my hope, wishing to send my wife out of my sight. But I am using stratagems, and finding contrivances against those I best love, overcome at all points. But nevertheless with the prophet Calchas I will go and ask the pleasure of the Goddess, not fortunate for me, the trouble of Greece. But it behooves a wise man either to support a useful and good wife in his house or not to marry at all.

CHORUS
The assembly of the Grecian army will come to Simois, and to the silver eddies, both with ships and with arms, to Ilium, and to the Phœbeian plain of Troy, where I hear that Cassandra, adorned with a green-blossoming crown of laurel, lets loose her yellow locks, when the prophetic influence of the Gods breathes upon her. And the Trojans will stand upon the towers of Troy and around its walls, when brazen-shielded Mars, borne over the sea in fair-prowed ships, approaches the beds of Simois by rowing, seeking to bear away Helen, the sister of the twain sons of Jove in heaven, into the land of Greece, by the war-toiling shields and spears of the Greeks. But having surrounded Pergamus, the city of the Phrygians, around its towers of stone, with bloody Mars, having torn off the heads of the

citizens cut from their necks, having completely ravaged the city of Troy, he will make the daughters and wife of Priam shed many tears. But Helen, the daughter of Jove, will sit in sad lamentation, having left her husband. Never upon me or upon my children's children may this expectation come, such as the wealthy Lydian and Phrygian wives possess while at their spinning, conversing thus with each other. Who, dragging out my fair-haired tresses, will choose me as his spoil despite my tears, while my country is perishing? Through thee forsooth, the offspring of the long-necked swan, if indeed the report is true, that Leda met with a winged bird, when the body of Jove was transformed, and then in the tablets of the muses fables spread these reports among men, inopportunely, and in vain.

[Enter **ACHILLES**.

ACHILLES
Where about here is the general of the Greeks? Who of the servants will tell him that Achilles, the son of Peleus, is seeking him at the gates? For we do not remain by the Euripus in equal condition; for some of us being unyoked in nuptials, having left our solitary homes, sit here upon the shore, but others, having wives and children: so violent a passion for this expedition has fallen upon Greece, not without the will of the Gods. It is therefore right that I should speak of what concerns me, and whoever else wishes will himself speak for himself. For leaving the Pharsalian land, and Peleus, I am waiting for these light gales of Euripus, restraining the Myrmidons, who are continually pressing me, and saying, "Achilles, why tarry we? what manner of time must the armament against Troy yet measure out? At any rate act, if you are going to do any thing, or lead the army home, not abiding the delays of the Atrides."

CLYTÆMNESTRA
O son of the Goddess, daughter of Nereus, hearing from within thy words, I have come out before the house.

ACHILLES
O hallowed modesty, who can this woman be whom I behold here, possessing a fair-seeming form?

CLYTÆMNESTRA
It is no wonder that you know me not, whom you have never seen before, but I commend you because you respect modesty.

ACHILLES
But who art thou? And wherefore hast thou come to the assembly of the Greeks, a woman to men guarded with shields?

CLYTÆMNESTRA
I am the daughter of Leda, and Clytæmnestra is my name, and my husband is king Agamemnon.

ACHILLES
Well hast thou in few words spoken what is seasonable. But it is unbecoming for me to converse with women.

[Is going.

CLYTÆMNESTRA
Remain, (why dost thou fly?) at least join thy right hand with mine, as a happy commencement of betrothal.

ACHILLES

What sayest thou? I give thee my right hand? I should be ashamed of Agamemnon, if I touched what is not lawful for me.

CLYTÆMNESTRA

It is particularly lawful, since you are going to wed my daughter, O son of the sea Goddess, daughter of Nereus.

ACHILLES

What marriage dost thou say? Surprise possesses me, lady, unless, being beside yourself, you speak this new thing.

CLYTÆMNESTRA

This is the nature of all people, to be ashamed when they behold new friends, and are put in mind of nuptials.

ACHILLES

I never wooed thy daughter, lady, nor has any thing been said to me on the subject of marriage by the Atrides.

CLYTÆMNESTRA

What can it be? Do you in turn marvel at my words, for thine are a marvel to me.

ACHILLES

Conjecture; these matters are a common subject for conjecture, for both of us perhaps are deceived in our words.

CLYTÆMNESTRA

But surely I have suffered terrible things! I am acting as match-maker in regard to a marriage that has no existence. I am ashamed of this.

ACHILLES

Perhaps some one has trifled with both me and thee. But pay no attention to it, and bear it with indifference.

CLYTÆMNESTRA

Farewell, for I can no longer behold thee with uplifted eyes, having appeared as a liar, and suffered unworthy things.

ACHILLES

And this same farewell is thine from me. But I will go seek thy husband within this house.

[The **OLD MAN** appears at the door of the house.

OLD MAN

O stranger, grandson of Æacus, remain. Ho! thee, I say, the son of the Goddess, and thee, the daughter of Leda.

ACHILLES

Who is it that calls, partially opening the doors? With what terror he calls!

OLD MAN

A slave. I will not be nice about the title, for fortune allows it not.

ACHILLES

Of whom? for thou art not mine. My property and Agamemnon's are different.

OLD MAN

Of this lady who is before the house, the gift of her father Tyndarus.

ACHILLES

We are still. Say if thou wantest any thing, for which thou hast stopped me.

OLD MAN

Are ye sure that ye alone stand before these gates?

CLYTÆMNESTRA

Ay, so that you may speak to us only. But come out from the royal dwelling.

OLD MAN [Coming forward]

O fortune, and foresight mine, preserve whom I wish.

ACHILLES

These words will do for a future occasion, for they have some weight.

CLYTÆMNESTRA

By thy right hand I beseech thee, delay not, if thou hast aught to say to me.

OLD MAN

Thou knowest then, being what manner of man, I have been by nature well disposed to thee and thy children.

CLYTÆMNESTRA

I know thee as being a faithful servant to my house.

OLD MAN

And that king Agamemnon received me among thy dowry.

CLYTÆMNESTRA

Thou camest into Argos with us, and thou wast always mine.

OLD MAN

So it is, and I am well disposed to thee, but less so to thy husband.

CLYTÆMNESTRA

Unfold now at least to me what words you are saying.

OLD MAN

The father who begat her is about to slay thy daughter with his own hand.

CLYTÆMNESTRA

How? I deprecate thy words, old man, for thou thinkest not well.

OLD MAN
Cutting the fair neck of the hapless girl with the sword.

CLYTÆMNESTRA
O wretched me! Is my husband mad?

OLD MAN
He is in his right mind, save with respect to thee and thy daughter, but in this he is not wise.

CLYTÆMNESTRA
Upon what grounds? What maddening fiend impels him?

OLD MAN
The oracles, as at least Calchas says, in order that the army may be able to proceed.

CLYTÆMNESTRA
Whither? Wretched me, and wretched she whom her father is about to slay?

OLD MAN
To the house of Dardanus, that Menelaus may recover Helen.

CLYTÆMNESTRA
To the destruction, then, of Iphigenia, was the return of Helen foredoomed?

OLD MAN
Thou hast the whole story. Her father is going to offer thy daughter to Diana.

CLYTÆMNESTRA
What! what pretext had the marriage, that brought me from home?

OLD MAN
That thou rejoicing mightest bring thy child, as if about to wed her to Achilles.

CLYTÆMNESTRA
O daughter, both thou and thy mother are come to meet with destruction.

OLD MAN
Ye twain are suffering sad things, and dreadful things hath Agamemnon dared.

CLYTÆMNESTRA
I wretched am undone, and my eyes no longer restrain the tear.

OLD MAN
For bitter 'tis to mourn, deprived of one's children.

CLYTÆMNESTRA
But whence, old man, sayest thou that thou hast learned and knowest these things?

OLD MAN

I went to bear a letter to thee, in reference to what was before written.

CLYTÆMNESTRA
Not allowing, or bidding me to bring my child, that she might die?

OLD MAN
It was that you should not bring her, for your husband then thought well.

CLYTÆMNESTRA
And how was it then, that, bearing the letter, thou gavest it not to me?

OLD MAN
Menelaus, who is the cause of these evils, took it from me.

CLYTÆMNESTRA
O child of Nereus' daughter, O son of Peleus, dost hear these things?

ACHILLES
I hear that thou art wretched, and I do not bear my part
indifferently.

CLYTÆMNESTRA
They will slay my child, having deceived her with thy nuptials.

ACHILLES
I also blame thy husband, nor do I bear it lightly.

CLYTÆMNESTRA
I will not be ashamed to fall down at thy knee, mortal, to one born of a Goddess. For wherefore should I make a show of pride? Or what should I study more than my children? But, O son of the Goddess, aid me in my unhappiness, and her who is called thy wife, vainly indeed, but nevertheless, having decked her out, I led her as if to be married, but now I lead her to sacrifice, and reproach will come upon thee, who gavest no aid. For though thou wast not yoked in nuptials, at least thou wast called the beloved husband of the hapless virgin. By thy beard, by thy right hand, by thy mother I beseech thee, for thy name hath undone me, to whom thou shouldst needs give assistance. I have no other altar to fly to, but thy knee, nor is any friend near me, but thou hearest the cruel and all-daring conduct of Agamemnon. But I a woman, as thou seest, have come to a naval host, uncontrolled, and bold for mischief, but useful, when they are willing. But if thou wilt venture to stretch thine hand in my behalf, we are saved, but if not, we are not saved.

CHORUS
A terrible thing it is to be a mother, and it bears a great endearment, and one common to all, so as to toil on behalf of their children.

ACHILLES
My mind is high-lifted in its thoughts, and knows both how to grieve moderately in troubles, and to rejoice moderately in high prosperity. For the discreet among mortals are such as pass through life correctly with wisdom. Now there are certain cases where it is pleasant not to be too wise, and also where it is useful to possess wisdom. But I, being nurtured in the dwelling of a most pious man, Chiron, have learned to possess a candid disposition. And I will obey the Atrides, if indeed they order well, but when not well, I obey not. But here in Troy showing a free nature I will glorify Mars with

the spear, as far as I can. But, O thou who hast suffered wretchedly at the hands of those dearest, in whatever can be done by a youth, I, showing so much pity, will set thee right, and thy daughter, having been called my bride, shall never be sacrificed by her father, for I will not furnish thy husband with my person to weave stratagems upon. For my name, even if he lift not up the sword, will slay thy daughter, but thy husband is the cause. But my body is no longer pure, if on my account, and because of my marriage, there perish a virgin who has gone through sad and unbearable troubles, and has been marvelously and undeservedly ill treated. I were the worst man among the Greeks, I were of naught (but Menelaus would be among men), not as born from Peleus, but from some fiend, if my name acts the murderer for thy husband. By Nereus, nurtured in the damp waves, the father of Thetis, who begat me, king Agamemnon shall not lay hands on thy daughter, not so much as with a little finger, so as to touch her garments. I' faith, Sipylus, a fortress of barbarians, whence the royal generals trace their descent, shall be deemed a city, but the name of Phthia shall nowhere be named. And the seer Calchas will to his cost consecrate the sacrificial cakes and lustral waters. But what man is a prophet? who tells a few things true, but many falsely, when he has made a hit, but when he fails, is undone. These words are not spoken for the sake of my wedding, (ten thousand girls are hunting after alliance with me,) but because king Agamemnon has been guilty of insult toward me. But it behooved him to ask the use of my name from me, as an enticement for his daughter, and Clytæmnestra would have been most readily persuaded to give her daughter to me as a husband. And I would have given her up to the Greeks, if on this account their passage to Troy had been impeded: I would not have refused to augment the common interest of those with whom I set out on the expedition. But now I am held as of no account by the generals, and it is a matter of indifference whether I benefit them or not. Soon shall my sword witness, which, before death came against the Phrygians, I stained with spots of blood, whether any one shall take thy daughter from me. But keep quiet, I have appeared to thee as a most mighty God, though not a God, but nevertheless I will be such.

CHORUS
O son of Peleus, thou hast spoken both worthily of thyself, and of the marine deity, hallowed Goddess.

CLYTÆMNESTRA
Alas! how can I praise thee neither too much in words, nor, being deficient in this respect, not lose thy favor? For in a certain wise the praised dislike their praisers, if they praise too much. But I am ashamed at alleging pitiable words, being troubled in myself, while thou art not diseased with my ills. But in fact the good man has some reason, even though he be unconnected with them, for assisting the unfortunate. But pity us, for we have suffered pitiably; I, who, in the first place, thinking to have thee for a kinsman, cherished a vain hope.—Moreover, my child, by dying, might perchance become an omen to thy future bridals, which thou must needs avoid. But well didst thou speak both first and last, for, if thou art willing, my child will be saved. Dost wish that she embrace thy knee as a suppliant? Such conduct is not virgin-like, but if thou wilt, she shall come, with her noble face suffused with modesty. Or shall I obtain these things from thee, without her presence?

ACHILLES
Let her remain within doors, for with dignity she preserves her dignity.

CLYTÆMNESTRA
Yet one must needs have modesty only as far as circumstances allow.

ACHILLES
Do thou neither bring forth thy daughter into my sight, lady, not let us fall into reproach for inconsiderate conduct, for our assembled army, being idle from home occupations, loves evil and

slanderous talk. But at all events you will accomplish the same, whether you come to me as a suppliant, or do not supplicate, for a mighty contest awaits me, to release you from these evils. Wherefore, having heard one thing, be persuaded that I will not speak falsely. But if I speak falsely, and vainly amuse you, may I perish; but may I not perish, if I preserve the virgin.

CLYTÆMNESTRA
Mayest thou be blest, ever assisting the unhappy.

ACHILLES
Hear me then, that the matter may be well.

CLYTÆMNESTRA
What is this thou sayest? for one must listen to thee.

ACHILLES
Let us again persuade her father to be wiser.

CLYTÆMNESTRA
He is a coward, and fears the army too much.

ACHILLES
But words can conquer words.

CLYTÆMNESTRA
Chilly is the hope, but tell me what I must do.

ACHILLES
Beseech him first not to slay his child, but if he oppose this, you must come to me. For if he will be persuaded what you wish, there is no occasion for my efforts, for this very consent contains her safety. And I also shall appear in a better light with my friend, and the army will not blame me, if I transact matters by discretion rather than force. And if this turn out well, these things, even without my help, may turn out satisfactorily to thy friends and thyself.

CLYTÆMNESTRA
How wisely hast thou spoken! But what thou sayest must be done. But if I do not obtain what I seek, where shall I again see thee? Where must I wretched woman, coming, find thee an assistant in my troubles?

ACHILLES
We guards will watch thee when there is occasion, lest any one behold thee going in agitation through the host of the Greeks. But do not shame thy ancestral home, for Tyndarus is not worthy of an evil reputation, seeing he is great among the Greeks.

CLYTÆMNESTRA
These things shall be. Command; it is meet that I obey thee. But if there are Gods, you, being a just man, will receive a good reward; but if not, why should one toil?

CHORUS
What was that nuptial song that raised its strains on the Libyan reed, and with the dance-loving lyre, and the reedy syrinx, when o'er Pelion at the feast of the Gods the fair-haired muses, striking their feet with golden sandals against the ground, came to the wedding of Peleus, celebrating with

melodious sounds Thetis, and the son of Æacus, on the mountains of the Centaurs, through the Palian wood.

But the Dardan, Phrygian Ganymede, dear delight of Jove's bed, poured out the nectar in the golden depths of the goblets, and along the white sands the fifty daughters of Nereus, entwining in circles, adorned the nuptials of Nereus with the dance. But with darts of fir, and crowns of grass, the horse-mounted troop of the Centaurs came to the banquet of the Gods and the cup of Bacchus. And the Thessalian girls shouted loud, "O daughter of Nereus," and the prophet Phœbus, and Chiron, skilled in letters, declared, "Thou shalt bring forth a mighty light, who shall come to the Trojan land with Myrmidons armed with spear and shield, to burn the renowned city of Priam, around his body armed with a covering of golden arms wrought by Vulcan, having them as a gift from his Goddess Thetis, who begat him blessed." Then the deities celebrated the nuptials of the noble daughter of Nereus first, and of Peleus. But thee, O Iphigenia, they will crown on the head with flowery garlands, like as a pure spotted heifer from a rocky cave, making bloody the mortal throat of one not trained up with the pipe, nor amidst the songs of herdsmen, but as a bride prepared by thy mother for some one of the Argives. Where has the face of shame, or virtue any power to prevail? Since impiety indeed has influence, but virtue is left behind and disregarded by mortals, and lawlessness governs law, and it is a common struggle for mortals, lest any envy of the Gods befall.

CLYTÆMNESTRA
I have come out of the house to seek for my husband, who has been absent, and has quitted the house a long time. But my hapless daughter is in tears, casting forth many a change of complaint, having heard the death her father devises for her. But I was mindful of Agamemnon who is now coming hither, who will quickly be detected doing evil deeds against his own children.

AGAMEMNON
Daughter of Leda, opportunely have I found you without the house, that I may tell thee, apart from the virgin, words which it is not meet for those to hear who are about to marry.

CLYTÆMNESTRA
And what is it, on which your convenience lays hold?

AGAMEMNON
Send forth thy daughter from the house with her father, since the lustral waters are ready prepared, and the salt-cakes to scatter with the hands upon the purifying flame, and heifers, which needs must be slain in honor of the Goddess Diana before the marriage solemnities, a shedding of black gore.

CLYTÆMNESTRA
In words, indeed, thou speakest well, but for thy deeds, I know not how I may say thou speakest well. But come without, O daughter, for thou knowest all that thy father meditates, and beneath thy robes bring the child Orestes, thy brother. See, she is here present to obey thee. But the rest I will speak on her behalf and mine.

AGAMEMNON
Child, why weepest thou, and no longer beholdest me cheerfully, but fixing thy face upon the ground, keepest thy vest before it?

CLYTÆMNESTRA
Alas! What commencement of my sorrows shall I take? For I may use them all as first, both last, and middle throughout.

AGAMEMNON

But what is it? How all of you are come to one point with me, bearing disturbed and alarmed countenances.

CLYTÆMNESTRA

Wilt thou answer candidly, husband, if I ask thee?

AGAMEMNON

There needs no admonition: I would fain be questioned.

CLYTÆMNESTRA

Art thou going to slay thy child and mine?

AGAMEMNON

Ah! wretched things dost thou say, and thinkest what thou shouldst not.

CLYTÆMNESTRA

Keep quiet, and first in turn answer me that.

AGAMEMNON

But if thou askest likely things, thou wilt hear likely.

CLYTÆMNESTRA

I ask no other things, nor do thou answer me others.

AGAMEMNON

O revered destiny, and fate, and fortune mine!

CLYTÆMNESTRA

Ay, and mine too, and this child's, one of three unfortunates!

AGAMEMNON

But in what art thou wronged?

CLYTÆMNESTRA

Dost thou ask me this? This thy wit hath no wit.

AGAMEMNON

I am undone. My secret plans are betrayed.

CLYTÆMNESTRA

I know and have learned all that you are about to do to me, and the very fact of thy silence, and of thy groaning much, is a proof that you confess it. Do not take the trouble to say any thing.

AGAMEMNON

Behold, I am silent: for what need is there that, falsely speaking, I add shamelessness to misfortune?

CLYTÆMNESTRA

Listen, then, for I will unfold my story, and will no longer make use of riddles away from the purpose. In the first place, that I may first reproach thee with this—thou didst wed me unwilling, and obtain me by force, having slain Tantalus, my former husband, and having dashed my infant living to the ground, having torn him by force from my breast. And the twin sons of Jove, my brothers, glorying in their steeds, made war against thee but my old father Tyndarus saved you, when you had become a suppliant, and thou again didst possess me as a wife. When I, being reconciled to thee in respect to thy person and home, thou wilt bear witness how blameless a wife I was, both modest in respect to affection, and enriching thy house, so that thou both going within and without thy doors wast blessed. And 'tis a rare prize for a man to obtain such a wife, but there is no lack of getting a bad spouse. And I bear thee this son, besides three virgins, of one of whom thou art cruelly going to deprive me. And if any one ask thee on what account thou wilt slay her, say, what will you answer? or must I needs make your plea, "that Menelaus may obtain Helen?" A pretty custom, forsooth, that children must pay the price of a bad woman. We gain the most hateful things at the hand of those dearest. Come, if thou wilt set out, leaving me at home, and then wilt be a long time absent, what sort of feelings dost think I shall experience, when I behold every seat empty of this child's presence, and every virgin chamber empty, but myself sit in tears alone, ever mourning her in such strains as these: "My child, thy father, who begat thee, hath destroyed thee, himself, no other, the slayer, by no other hand, leaving such a reward for my care of the house." Since there wants but a little reason for me and my remaining daughters to give thee such a reception as you deserve to receive. Do not, by the Gods, either compel me to act evilly toward thee, nor do thou thyself be so. Ah well! thou wilt sacrifice thy daughter—what prayers wilt thou then utter? What good thing wilt thou crave for thyself, slaying thy child? An evil return, seeing, forsooth, thou hast disgracefully set out from home. But is it right that I should pray for thee any good thing? Verily we must believe the Gods are senseless, if we feel well disposed to murderers. But wilt thou, returning to Argos, embrace thy children? But 'tis not lawful for thee. Will any of your children look upon you, if thou offerest one of them for slaughter? Thus far have I proceeded in my argument. What! does it only behoove thee to carry about thy sceptre and marshal the army?—whose duty it were to speak a just speech among the Greeks: "Do ye desire, O Greeks, to sail against the land of the Phrygians? Cast lots, whose daughter needs must die"—for this would be on equal terms, but not that you should give thy daughter to the Greeks as a chosen victim. Or Menelaus, whose affair it was, ought to slay Hermione for her mother's sake. But now I, having cherished thy married life, shall be bereaved of my child, but she who has sinned, bearing her daughter under her care to Sparta, will be blest. As to these things, answer me if I say aught not rightly, but if I have spoken well, do not then slay thy child and mine, and thou wilt be wise.

CHORUS
Be persuaded, Agamemnon, for 'tis right to join in saving one's children. No one of mortals will gainsay this.

IPHIGENIA
If, O father, I possessed the eloquence of Orpheus, that I might charm by persuasion, so that rocks should follow me, and that I might soften whom I would by my words, to this would I have resorted. But now I will offer tears as all my skill, for these I can. And, as a suppliant bough, I press against thy knees my body, which this my mother bore thee, beseeching that thou slay me not before my time, for sweet it is to behold the light, nor do thou compel me to visit the places beneath the earth. And I first hailed thee sire, and thou didst first call me daughter, and first drawing nigh to thy knees, I gave and in turn received sweet tokens of affection. And such, were thy words: "My daughter, shall I some time behold thee prospering in a husband's home, living and flourishing worthily of me?" And mine in turn ran thus, as I hung about thy beard, which now with my hand I embrace: "But how shall I treat thee? Shall I receive thee when an old man, O father, with the hearty reception of my house, repaying thee the careful nurture of my youth?" Of such words have remembrance, but thou hast forgotten them, and fain wouldst slay me. Do not, I beseech you by Pelops and by thy father Atreus, and this my mother, who having before brought me forth with throes, now suffers this second throe. What have I to do with the marriage of Paris and Helen? Whence came he, father, for my

destruction? Look upon me; give me one look, one kiss, that this memorial of thee at least I, dying, may possess, if thou wilt not be persuaded by my words. Brother, thou art but a little helpmate to those dear, yet weep with me, beseech thy sire that thy sister die not. Even in babes there is wont to be some sense of evil. Behold, O father, he silently implores thee. But respect my prayer, and have pity on my years. Yea, by thy beard we, two dear ones, implore thee; the one is yet a nursling, but the other grown up. In one brief saying I will overcome all arguments. This light of heaven is sweetest of things for men to behold, but that below is naught; and mad is he who seeks to die. To live dishonorably is better than to die gloriously.

CHORUS
O wretched Helen, through thee and thy nuptials there is come a contest for the Atrides and their children.

AGAMEMNON
I can understand what merits pity, and what not; and I love my children, for otherwise I were mad. And dreadful 'tis for me to dare these things, O woman, and dreadful not to do so—for so I must needs act. Thou seest how great is this naval host, and how many are the chieftains of brazen arms among the Greeks, to whom there is not a power of arriving at the towers of Troy, unless I sacrifice you, as the seer Calchas says, nor can we take the renowned plain of Troy. But a certain passion has maddened the army of the Greeks, to sail as quickly as possible upon the land of the barbarians, and to put a stop to the rapes of Grecian wives. And they will slay my daughters at Argos, and you, and me, if I break through the commands of the Goddess. It is not Menelaus who has enslaved me, O daughter, nor have I followed his device, but Greece, for whom I, will or nill, must needs offer thee. And I am inferior on this head. For it behooves her, Helen, as far as thou, O daughter, art concerned, to be free, nor for us, being Greeks, to be plundered perforce of our wives by barbarians.

CLYTÆMNESTRA
O child! O ye stranger women! O wretched me for thy death! Thy father flees from thee, giving thee up to Hades.

IPHIGENIA
Alas for me! mother, mother. The same song suits both of us on account of our fortunes, and no more to me is the light, nor this bright beam of the sun. Alas! alas! thou snow-smitten wood of Troy, and mountains of Ida, where once on a time Priam exposed a tender infant, having separated him from his mother, that he might meet with deadly fate, Paris, who was styled Idæan, Idæan Paris in the city of the Phrygians. Would that the herdsman Paris, who was nurtured in care of steers, had ne'er dwelt near the white stream, where are the fountains of the Nymphs, and the meadow flourishing with blooming flowers, and roseate flowers and hyacinths for Goddesses to cull. Where once on a time came Pallas, and artful Venus, and Juno, and Hermes, the messenger of Jove; Venus indeed, vaunting herself in charms, and Pallas in the spear, and Juno in the royal nuptials of king Jove, these came to a hateful judgment and strife concerning beauty; but my death, my death, O virgins, bearing glory indeed to the Greeks, Diana hath received as first-fruits of the expedition against Troy. But he that begot me wretched, O mother, O mother, has departed, leaving me deserted. O hapless me! having beheld bitter, bitter, ill-omened Helen, I am slain, I perish, by the impious slaughter of an impious sire. Would for me that Aulis had never received the poops of the brazen-beaked ships into these ports, the fleet destined for Troy, nor that Jove had breathed an adverse wind over Euripus, softening one breeze so that some mortals might rejoice in their expanded sails, but to others a pain, to others difficulty, to some to set sail, to others to furl their sails, but to others to tarry. In truth the race of mortals is full of troubles, is full of troubles, and it necessarily befalls men to find some misfortune. Alas! alas! thou daughter of Tyndarus, who hast brought many sufferings, and many griefs upon the Greeks.

CHORUS
I indeed pity you having met with an evil calamity, such as thou never shouldst have met with.

IPHIGENIA
O mother, to whom I owe my birth, I behold a crowd of men near.

CLYTÆMNESTRA
Ay, the son of the Goddess, my child, for whom thou camest hither.

IPHIGENIA
Open the house, ye servants, that I may hide myself.

CLYTÆMNESTRA
But why dost thou fly hence, my child?

IPHIGENIA
I am ashamed to behold this Achilles.

CLYTÆMNESTRA
On what account?

IPHIGENIA
The unfortunate turn-out of my nuptials shames me.

CLYTÆMNESTRA
Thou art not in a state to give way to delicacy in the present circumstances. But do thou remain, there is no use for punctilio, if we can but save your life.

ACHILLES
O hapless lady, daughter of Leda.

CLYTÆMNESTRA
Thou sayest not falsely.

ACHILLES
Terrible things are cried out among the Greeks.

CLYTÆMNESTRA
What cry? tell me.

ACHILLES
Concerning thy child.

CLYTÆMNESTRA
Thou speakest a word of ill omen.

ACHILLES
That it is necessary to slay her.

CLYTÆMNESTRA

Does no one speak the contrary to this?

ACHILLES
Ay, I myself have got into trouble.

CLYTÆMNESTRA
Into what trouble, O friend?

ACHILLES
Of having my body stoned with stones.

CLYTÆMNESTRA
What, in trying to save my daughter!

ACHILLES
This very thing.

CLYTÆMNESTRA
And who would have dared to touch thy person?

ACHILLES
All the Greeks.

CLYTÆMNESTRA
And was not the host of the Myrmidons at hand for thee?

ACHILLES
That was the first that showed enmity.

CLYTÆMNESTRA
Then are we utterly undone, my daughter.

ACHILLES
For they railed at me as overcome by a betrothed—

CLYTÆMNESTRA
And what didst thou reply?

ACHILLES
That they should not slay my intended bride.

CLYTÆMNESTRA
For so 'twas right.

ACHILLES
She whom her father had promised me.

CLYTÆMNESTRA
Ay, and had sent for from Argos.

ACHILLES

But I was worsted by the outcry.

CLYTÆMNESTRA
For the multitude is a terrible evil.

ACHILLES
But nevertheless I will aid thee.

CLYTÆMNESTRA
And wilt thou, being one, fight with many?

ACHILLES
Dost see these men bearing my arms?

CLYTÆMNESTRA
Mayest thou gain by thy good intentions.

ACHILLES
But I will gain.

CLYTÆMNESTRA
Then my child will not be slain?

ACHILLES
Not, at least, with my consent.

CLYTÆMNESTRA
And will any one come to lay hands on the girl?

ACHILLES
Ay, a host of them, but Ulysses will conduct her.

CLYTÆMNESTRA
Will it be the descendant of Sisyphus?

ACHILLES
The very man.

CLYTÆMNESTRA
Doing it of his own accord, or appointed by the army?

ACHILLES
Chosen willingly.

CLYTÆMNESTRA
A wicked choice forsooth, to commit slaughter!

ACHILLES
But I will restrain him.

CLYTÆMNESTRA

But will he lead her unwillingly, having seized her?

ACHILLES
Ay, by her auburn locks.

CLYTÆMNESTRA
But what must I then do?

ACHILLES
Keep hold of your daughter.

CLYTÆMNESTRA
As far as this goes she shall not be slain.

ACHILLES
But it will come to this at all events.

IPHIGENIA
Mother, do thou hear my words, for I perceive that thou art vainly wrathful with thy husband, but it is not easy for us to struggle with things almost impossible. It is meet therefore to praise our friend for his willingness, but it behooves thee also to see that you be not an object of reproach to the army, and we profit nothing more, and he meet with calamity. But hear me, mother, thinking upon what has entered my mind. I have determined to die, and this I would fain do gloriously, I mean, by dismissing all ignoble thoughts. Come hither, mother, consider with me how well I speak. Greece, the greatest of cities, is now all looking upon me, and there rests in me both the passage of the ships and the destruction of Troy, and, for the women hereafter, if the barbarians do them aught of harm, to allow them no longer to carry them off from prosperous Greece, having avenged the destruction of Helen, whom Paris bore away. All these things I dying shall redeem, and my renown, for that I have freed Greece, will be blessed. Moreover, it is not right that I should be too fond of life; for thou hast brought me forth for the common good of Greece, not for thyself only. But shall ten thousand men armed with bucklers, and ten thousand, oars in hand, their country being injured, dare to do some deed against the foes, and perish on behalf of Greece, while my life, being but one, shall hinder all these things? What manner of justice is this? Have we a word to answer? And let me come to this point: it is not meet that this man should come to strife with all the Greeks for the sake of a woman, nor lose his life. And one man, forsooth, is better than ten thousand women, that he should behold the light. But if Diana hath wished to receive my body, shall I, being mortal, become an opponent to the Goddess! But it can not be. I give my body for Greece. Sacrifice it, and sack Troy. For this for a long time will be my memorial, and this my children, my wedding, and my glory. But it is meet that Greeks should rule over barbarians, O mother, but not barbarians over Greeks, for the one is slavish, but the others are free.

CHORUS
Thy part, indeed, O virgin, is glorious; but the work of fortune and of the Gods sickens.

ACHILLES
Daughter of Agamemnon, some one of the Gods destined me to happiness, if I obtained thee as a wife, and I envy Greece on thy account, and thee on account of Greece. For well hast thou spoken this, and worthily of the country, for, ceasing to strive with the deity, who is more powerful than thou art, thou hast considered what is good and useful. But still more does a desire of thy union enter my mind, when I look to thy nature, for thou art noble. But consider, for I wish to benefit you,

and to receive you to my home, and, Thetis be my witness, I am grieved if I shall not save you, coming to conflict with the Greeks. Consider: death is a terrible ill.

IPHIGENIA
I speak these words, no others, with due foresight. Enough is the daughter of Tyndarus to have caused contests and slaughter of men through her person: but do not thou, O stranger, die in my behalf, nor slay any one. But let me preserve Greece, if I am able.

ACHILLES
O best of spirits, I have naught further to answer thee, since it seems thus to thee, for thou hast noble thoughts; for wherefore should not one tell the truth? But nevertheless thou mayest perchance repent these things. In order, therefore, that thou mayest all that lies in my power, I will go and place these my arms near the altar, as I will not allow you to die, but hinder it. And thou too wilt perhaps be of my opinion, when thou seest the sword nigh to thy neck. I will not allow thee to die through thy wild determination, but going with these mine arms to the temple of the Goddess, I will await thy presence there.

IPHIGENIA
Mother, why dost thou silently bedew thine eyes with tears?

CLYTÆMNESTRA
I wretched have a reason, so as to be pained at heart.

IPHIGENIA
Cease; do not daunt me, but obey me in this.

CLYTÆMNESTRA
Speak, for thou shalt not be wronged at my hands, my child.

IPHIGENIA
Neither then do thou cut off the locks of thine hair, nor put on black garments around thy body.

CLYTÆMNESTRA
Wherefore sayest thou this, my child? Having lost thee—

IPHIGENIA
Not you indeed—I am saved, and thou wilt be glorious as far as I am concerned.

CLYTÆMNESTRA
How sayest thou? Must I not bemoan thy life?

IPHIGENIA
Not in the least, since no tomb will be upraised for me.

CLYTÆMNESTRA
Why, what then is death? Is not a tomb customary?

IPHIGENIA
The altar of the Goddess, daughter of Jove, will be my memorial.

CLYTÆMNESTRA

But, O child, I will obey thee, for thou speakest well.

IPHIGENIA
Ay, as prospering like the benefactress of Greece.

CLYTÆMNESTRA
What then shall I tell thy sisters?

IPHIGENIA
Neither do thou clothe them in black garments.

CLYTÆMNESTRA
But shall I speak any kind message from thee to the virgins?

IPHIGENIA
Ay, bid them fare well, and do thou, for my sake, train up this boy Orestes to be a man.

CLYTÆMNESTRA
Embrace him, beholding him for the last time.

IPHIGENIA
O dearest one, thou hast assisted thy friends to the utmost in thy power.

CLYTÆMNESTRA
Can I, by doing any thing in Argos, do thee a pleasure?

IPHIGENIA
Hate not my father, yes, thy husband.

CLYTÆMNESTRA
He needs shall go through terrible trials on thy account.

IPHIGENIA
Unwillingly he hath undone me on behalf of the land of Greece.

CLYTÆMNESTRA
But ungenerously, by craft, and not in a manner worthy of Atreus.

IPHIGENIA
Who will come and lead me, before I am torn away by the hair?

CLYTÆMNESTRA
I will go with thee.

IPHIGENIA
Not you indeed, thou sayest not well.

CLYTÆMNESTRA
Ay but I will, clinging to thy garments.

IPHIGENIA

Be persuaded by me, mother. Remain, for this is more fitting both for me and thee. But let some one of these my father's followers conduct me to the meadow of Diana, where I may be sacrificed.

CLYTÆMNESTRA
O child, thou art going.

IPHIGENIA
Ay, and I shall ne'er return.

CLYTÆMNESTRA
Leaving thy mother—

IPHIGENIA
As thou seest, though, not worthily.

CLYTÆMNESTRA
Hold! Do not leave me.

IPHIGENIA
I do not suffer thee to shed tears. But, ye maidens, raise aloft the pæan for my sad hap, celebrate Diana, the daughter of Jove,95 and let the joyful strain go forth to the Greeks. And let some one make ready the baskets, and let flame burn with the purifying cakes, and let my father serve the altar with his right hand, seeing I am going to bestow upon the Greeks safety that produces victory.

Conduct me, the conqueror of the cities of Troy and of the Phrygians. Surround me with crowns, bring them hither. Here is my hair to crown. And bear hither the lustral fountains. Encircle with dances around the temple and the altar, Diana, queen Diana, the blessed, since by my blood and offering I will wash out her oracles, if it needs must be so. O revered, revered mother, thus indeed will we now afford thee our tears, for it is not fitting during the sacred rites. O damsels, join in singing Diana, who dwells opposite Chalcis, where the warlike ships have been eager to set out, being detained in the narrow harbors of Aulis here through my name. Alas! O my mother-land of Pelasgia, and my Mycenian handmaids.

CHORUS
Dost thou call upon the city of Perseus, the work of the Cyclopean hands?

IPHIGENIA
Thou hast nurtured me for a glory to Greece, and I will not refuse to die.

CHORUS
For renown will not fail thee.

IPHIGENIA
Alas! alas! lamp-bearing day, and thou too, beam of Jove, another, another life and state shall we dwell in. Farewell for me, beloved light!

CHORUS
Alas! alas! Behold the destroyer of the cities of Troy and of the Phrygians, wending her way, decked as to her head with garlands and with lustral streams, to the altar of the sanguinary Goddess, about to stream with drops of gore, being stricken on her fair neck. Fair dewy streams, and lustral waters from ancestral sources await thee, and the host of the Greeks eager to reach Troy. But let us

celebrate Diana, the daughter of Jove, queen of the Gods, as upon a prosperous occasion. O hallowed one, that rejoicest in human sacrifices, send the army of the Greeks into the land of the Phrygians, and the territory of deceitful Troy, and grant that by Grecian spears Agamemnon may place a most glorious crown upon his head, a glory ever to be remembered.

[Enter a **MESSENGER**.

MESSENGER
O daughter of Tyndarus, Clytæmnestra, come without the house, that thou mayest hear my words.

CLYTÆMNESTRA
Hearing thy voice, I wretched came hither, terrified and astounded with fear, lest thou shouldst be come, bearing some new calamity to me in addition to the present one.

MESSENGER
Concerning thy daughter, then, I wish to tell thee marvelous and fearful things.

CLYTÆMNESTRA
Then delay not, but speak as quickly as possible.

MESSENGER
But, my dear mistress, thou shalt learn every thing clearly, and I will speak from the very commencement, unless my memory, in something failing, deceive my tongue. For when we came to the inclosure and flowery meads of Diana, the daughter of Jove, where there was an assembly of the army of the Greeks, leading thy daughter, the host of the Greeks was straightway convened. But when king Agamemnon beheld the girl wending her way to the grove for slaughter, he groaned aloud, and turning back his head, he shed tears, placing his garments before his eyes. But she, standing near him that begot her, spake thus: "O father, I am here for thee, and I willing give my body on behalf of my country, and of the whole land of Greece, that, leading it to the altar of the Goddess, they may sacrifice it, since this is ordained. And, as far as I am concerned, may ye be fortunate, and obtain the gift of victory, and reach your native land. Furthermore, let no one of the Greeks lay hands on me, for with a stout heart I will present my neck in silence." Thus much she spoke, and every one marveled on hearing the courage and valor of the virgin. But Talthybius, whose office this was, standing in the midst, proclaimed good-omened silence to the people. And the seer Calchas placed in a golden canister a sharp knife, which he had drawn out, within its case, and crowned the head of the girl. But the son of Peleus ran around the altar of the Goddess, taking the canister and lustral waters at the same time. And he said: "O Diana, beast-slaying daughter of Jove, that revolvest thy brilliant light by night, receive this offering which we bestow on thee, we the army of the Greeks, and king Agamemnon, the pure blood from a fair virgin's neck; and grant that the sail may be without injury to our ships, and that we may take the towers of Troy by the spear." But the Atrides and all the army stood looking on the ground, and the priest, taking the knife, prayed, and viewed her neck, that he might find a place to strike. And no little pity entered my mind, and I stood with eyes cast down, but suddenly there was a marvel to behold. For every one could clearly perceive the sound of the blow, but beheld not the virgin, where on earth she had vanished. But the priest exclaimed, and the whole army shouted, beholding an unexpected prodigy from some one of the Gods, of which, though seen, they had scarcely belief. For a stag lay panting on the ground, of mighty size to see and beautiful in appearance, with whose blood the altar of the Goddess was abundantly wetted. And upon this Calchas (think with what joy!) thus spake: "O leaders of this common host of the Greeks, behold this victim which the Goddess hath brought to her altar, a mountain-roaming stag. This she prefers greatly to the virgin, lest her altar should be denied with generous blood. And she hath willingly received this, and grants us a prosperous sail, and attack

upon Troy. Upon this do every sailor take good courage, and go to his ships, since on this day it behooves us, quitting the hollow recesses of Aulis, to pass over the Ægean wave." But when the whole victim was reduced to ashes, he prayed what was meet, that the army might obtain a passage. And Agamemnon sends me to tell thee this, and to say what a fortune he hath met with from the Gods, and hath obtained unwaning glory through Greece. But I speak, having been present, and witnessing the matter. Thy child has evidently flown to the Gods; away then with grief, and cease wrath against your husband. But the will of the Gods is unforeseen by mortals, and them they love, they save. For this day hath beheld thy daughter dying and living in turn.

CHORUS
How delighted am I at hearing this from the messenger; but he says that thy daughter living abides among the Gods.

CLYTÆMNESTRA
O daughter, of whom of the Gods art thou the theft? How shall I address thee? What shall I say that these words do not offer me a vain comfort, that I may cease from my mournful grief on thy account?

CHORUS
And truly king Agamemnon draws hither, having this same story to tell thee.

[Enter **AGAMEMNON**.

AGAMEMNON
Lady, as far as thy daughter is concerned, we may be happy, for she really possesses a companionship with the Gods. But it behooves thee, taking this young child Orestes, to go home, for the army is looking toward setting sail. And fare thee well, long hence will be my addresses to thee from Troy, and may it be well with thee.

CHORUS
Atrides, rejoicing go thou to the land of the Phrygians, and rejoicing return, having obtained for me most glorious spoils from Troy.

Euripides – A Short Biography

Euripides is rightly lauded as one of the great dramatists of all time. In his lifetime, he wrote over 90 plays and although only 18 have survived they reveal the scope and reach of his genius.

Euripides is identified with many theatrical innovations that have influenced drama all the way down to modern times, especially in the representation of traditional, mythical heroes as ordinary people in extraordinary circumstances. This new approach led him to pioneer developments that later writers would adapt to comedy. Yet he also became "the most tragic of poets", focusing on the inner lives and motives of his characters in a way previously unknown. He was "the creator of...that cage which is the theatre of Shakespeare's Othello, Racine's Phèdre, of Ibsen and Strindberg," in which "...imprisoned men and women destroy each other by the intensity of their loves and hates", and yet he was also the literary ancestor of comic dramatists as diverse as Menander and George Bernard Shaw.

As would be expected from a life lived 2,500 years ago, details of it are few and far between. Accounts of his life, written down the ages, do exist but whether much is reliable or surmised is open to debate.

Most accounts agree that he was born on Salamis Island around 480 BC, to mother Cleito and father Mnesarchus, a retailer who lived in a village near Athens. Upon the receipt of an oracle saying that his son was fated to win "crowns of victory", Mnesarchus insisted that the boy should train for a career in athletics.

His education was not only confined to athletics: he also studied painting and philosophy under the masters Prodicus and Anaxagoras.

However, what became quickly very clear was that athletics was not to be his way to win crowns of victory. Euripides had been lucky enough to have been born in the era as the other two masters of Greek Tragedy; Sophocles and Æschylus. It was in their footsteps that he was destined to follow.

His first play was performed some thirteen years after the first of Socrates plays and a mere three years after Æschylus had written his classic The Oristria.

Theatre was becoming a very important part of the Greek culture. The Dionysia, held annually, was the most important festival of theatre and second only to the fore-runner of the Olympic games, the Panathenia, held every four years, in its appeal. It was a large festival in ancient Athens in honor of the god Dionysus, the central events of which were the theatrical performances of dramatic tragedies and, from 487 BC, comedies. The Dionysia actually consisted of two related festivals, the Rural Dionysia and the City Dionysia, which took place in different parts of the year.

Euripides first competed in the City Dionysia, in 455 BC, one year after the death of Æschylus, and, incredibly, it was not until 441 BC that he won first prize. His final competition in Athens was in 408 BC. However, The Bacchae and Iphigenia in Aulis were performed after his death in 405 BC and first prize was awarded posthumously. Altogether his plays won first prize only five times.

His plays, and those of Æschylus and Sophocles, indicate a difference in outlook between the three men, most easily explained as a generational gap, although with three great talents overlapping the driving forces may have pushed individual styles onwards perhaps faster than they may otherwise have done. Æschylus still looked back to the archaic period, Sophocles was in transition between periods, and Euripides was fully bonded with the new spirit of the classical age. When Euripides' plays are sequenced in time, they also show a developing pattern:

An early period of high tragedy (Medea, Hippolytus)
A patriotic period at the outset of the Peloponnesian War (Children of Hercules, Suppliants)
A middle period of disillusionment at the senselessness of war (Hecuba, Women of Troy)
An escapist period with a focus on romantic intrigue (Ion, Iphigenia in Tauris, Helen)
A final period of tragic despair (Orestes, Phoenician Women, Bacchae)

However, with over three quarters of his plays lost it is difficult to be certain as to whether the other works would also represent this development (e.g., Iphigenia at Aulis is dated with the 'despairing' Bacchae, yet it contains elements that became typical of New Comedy). In the Bacchae, he restores the chorus and messenger speech to their traditional role in the tragic plot, and the play appears to be the culmination of a regressive or archaizing tendency in his later works.

In one of his earliest surviving plays, Medea, includes a speech that he seems to have written in defence of himself as an intellectual ahead of his time, and to further challenge the times he has put the words in the mouth of the play's heroine:

"If you introduce new, intelligent ideas to fools, you will be thought frivolous, not intelligent. On the other hand, if you do get a reputation for surpassing those who are supposed to be intellectually sophisticated, you will seem to be a thorn in the city's flesh. This is what has happened to me."— Medea.

As we know Athenian tragedies during Euripides' lifetime were a public contest between playwrights. The state funded that contest and awarded prizes to the winners. The language was spoken and sung verse, the performance area included a circular floor or orchestra where the chorus could dance, a space for actors (usually three speaking actors in Euripides' time), a backdrop or skene and some special effects: an ekkyklema (used to bring the skene's "indoors" outdoors) and a mechane (used to lift actors in the air, as in deus ex machina). With the introduction of the third actor (an innovation attributed to Sophocles), acting also began to be regarded as a skill to be rewarded with prizes, requiring a long apprenticeship in the chorus. Euripides and other playwrights accordingly composed more and more arias for accomplished actors to sing and this tendency becomes more marked in his later plays: tragedy for him was a living and ever-changing genre.

Accounts by the famed comic poet, Aristophanes, characterise Euripides as a spokesman for destructive, new ideas, that mirror or help to bring about declining standards in both society and tragedy. However, 5th century tragedy was a social gathering for "carrying out quite publicly the maintenance and development of mental infrastructure" and it offered spectators a "platform for an utterly unique form of institutionalized discussion". A dramatist's role was not just to entertain but also to educate his fellow citizens—he was expected to have a message. Clearly this use of drama to democratize discussion was a very useful tool for all sides. Traditional myth provided the subject matter but the dramatist was meant to be innovative so as to sustain interest, which led to novel characterization of heroic figures and to use the mythical past to talk about present issues. The difference between Euripides and his older colleagues was, again, one of degree: his characters talked about the present more controversially and more pointedly than did those of Æschylus and Sophocles, sometimes even challenging the democratic order. Thus, for example, Odysseus is represented in Hecuba as "agile-minded, sweet-talking, demos-pleasing" i.e., a type of the war-time demagogues that were active in Athens during the Peloponnesian War. His concept is pleasingly simple. He retains the old stories and myths as well as the great names of the past and places them in the lives of contemporary Athenians thereby immediately help the audience understand it from the point of view of their own lives.

As mouthpieces for contemporary issues, they all seem to have had at least an elementary course in public speaking. Sometimes the dialogue often contrasts so strongly with the mythical and heroic setting, it looks as if Euripides aimed at parody, as for example in The Trojan Women, where the heroine's rationalized prayer provokes comment from Menelaus:

Hecuba:...O Zeus, whether you are the Law of Necessity in nature, or the Law of Reason in man, hear my prayers. You are everywhere, pursuing your noiseless path, ordering the affairs of mortals according to justice.

Menelaus: What's this? You are starting a new fashion in prayer.

Athenian citizens were familiar with rhetoric in the assembly and law courts, and some scholars believe that Euripides was more interested in his characters as speakers with cases to argue than as characters with lifelike personalities. They are self-conscious about speaking formally and their rhetoric is shown to be flawed, as if Euripides was exploring the problematical nature of language and communication: "For speech points in three different directions at once, to the speaker, to the person addressed, to the features in the world it describes, and each of these directions can be felt as skewed". Thus in the example above, Hecuba presents herself as a sophisticated intellectual describing a rationalised cosmos yet the speech is ill-matched to her audience, Menelaus (an unsophisticated listener), and soon it is found not to suit the cosmos either (her infant grandson is brutally murdered by the victorious Greeks).

Æschylus and Sophocles were innovative, but Euripides could move easily between tragic, comic, romantic and political effects, a versatility that appears in individual plays and also over the course of his career. Potential for comedy lay in his use of 'contemporary' characters, in his sophisticated tone, his relatively informal Greek, and his ingenious use of plots centered on motifs that later became standard, such as the 'recognition scene'. Other tragedians also used recognition scenes but they were heroic in emphasis, as in Æschylus's The Libation Bearers, which Euripides parodied with his mundane treatment of it in Electra (Euripides was unique among the tragedians in incorporating theatrical criticism in his plays). Traditional myth, with its exotic settings, heroic adventures and epic battles, offered potential for romantic melodrama as well as for political comments on a war theme, so that his plays are an extraordinary mix of elements. The Trojan Women for example is a powerfully disturbing play on the theme of war's horrors, apparently critical of Athenian imperialism (it was composed in the aftermath of the Melian massacre and during the preparations for the Sicilian Expedition) yet it features the comic exchange between Menelaus and Hecuba quoted above and the chorus considers Athens, the "blessed land of Theus", to be a desirable refuge—such complexity and ambiguity are typical both of his "patriotic" and "anti-war" plays.

Tragic poets in the 5th century competed against one another at the City Dionysia, each with a tetralogy consisting of three tragedies and a satyr-play. The few extant fragments of satyr-plays attributed to Æschylus and Sophocles indicate that these were a loosely structured, simple and jovial form of entertainment. However, in Cyclops (the only complete Euripides satyr-play that survives) the entertainment is structured more like a tragedy and introduced a note of critical irony typical of his other work. His genre-bending inventiveness is shown above all in Alcestis, a blend of tragic and satyric elements. This fourth play in his tetralogy for 438 BC (i.e., it occupied the position conventionally reserved for satyr-plays) is a "tragedy" that features Heracles as a satyric hero in conventional satyr-play scenes, involving an arrival, a banquet, a victory over an ogre (in this case, Death), a happy ending, a feast and a departure to new adventures.

Euripides was also a great lyric poet. In Medea, for example, he composed for his city, Athens, "the noblest of her songs of praise". His lyric skills however are not just confined to individual poems: "A play of Euripides is a musical whole....one song echoes motifs from the preceding song, while introducing new ones."

Much of his life and his whole career coincided with the struggle between Athens and Sparta for hegemony in Greece but he didn't live to see the final defeat of his city.

It is said that he died in Macedonia after being attacked by the Molossian hounds of King Archelaus and that his cenotaph near Piraeus was struck by lightning—signs of his unique powers, whether for good or ill. In an account by Plutarch, the complete failure of the Sicilian expedition led Athenians to trade renditions of Euripides' lyrics to their enemies in return for food and drink (Life of Nicias 29). Plutarch is the source also for the story that the victorious Spartan generals, having planned the demolition of Athens and the enslavement of its people, grew merciful after being entertained at a banquet by lyrics from Euripides' play Electra: "they felt that it would be a barbarous act to annihilate a city which produced such men" (Life of Lysander).

In The Frogs, composed after Euripides and Æschylus were both dead, Aristophanes imagines the god Dionysus venturing down to Hades in search of a good poet to bring back to Athens. After a debate between the two deceased bards, the god brings Æschylus back to life as more useful to Athens on account of his wisdom, rejecting Euripides as merely clever. Such comic 'evidence' suggests that Athenians admired Euripides even while they mistrusted his intellectualism, at least during the long war with Sparta.

Euripides had a famous library—one of the first to be privately collected. Although he lived most of his life in the midst of the cultured society of Athens, and was in some respects a leader in it, he grew bitter and despondent over the fierce rivalries and greedy ambitions which ran through the city. He loved the seclusion of his house at Salamis, where it was said that he composed his dramas in a cave.

Euripides fell out of favour with his fellow Athenian citizens and retired to the court of Archelaus, king of Macedon, who treated him with consideration and affection.

At his death, in around 406BC, he was mourned by the king, who, refusing the request of the Athenians that his remains be carried back to the Greek city, buried him with much splendor within his own dominions. His tomb was placed at the confluence of two streams, near Arethusa in Macedonia, and a cenotaph was built to his memory on the road from Athens towards the Piraeus.

Euripides – A Concise Bibliography

Alcestis (438 BC)
Medea (431 BC)
Heracleidae (c. 430 BC)
Hippolytus (428 BC)
Andromache (c. 425 BC)
Hecuba (c. 424 BC)
The Suppliants (c. 423 BC)
Electra (c. 420 BC)
Heracles (c. 416 BC)
The Trojan Women (c. 415 BC)
Iphigenia in Tauris (c. 414 BC)
Ion (c. 414 BC)
Helen (c. 412 BC)
Phoenician Women (c. 410 BC)
Orestes (c.408 BC)
Bacchae (405 BC)
Iphigenia at Aulis (405 BC)
Rhesus
Cyclops

Lost and Fragmentary Plays (Dated)

Peliades (455 BC)
Telephus (438 BC with Alcestis)
Alcmaeon in Psophis (438 BC with Alcestis)
Cretan Women (438 with Alcestis)
Cretans (c. 435 BC)
Philoctetes (431 BC with Medea)
Dictys (431 BC with Medea)
Theristai (satyr play, 431 BC with Medea)
Stheneboea (before 429 BC)
Bellerophon (c. 430 BC)
Cresphontes (ca. 425 BC)
Erechtheus (422 BC)
Phaethon (c. 420 BC)
Wise Melanippe (c. 420 BC)
Alexandros (415 BC with Trojan Women)
Palamedes (415 BC with Trojan Women)
Sisyphus (satyr play, 415 BC with Trojan Women)
Captive Melanippe (c. 412 BC)
Andromeda (412 BC with Helen)
Antiope (c. 410 BC)
Archelaus (c. 410 BC)
Hypsipyle (c. 410 BC)
Alcmaeon in Corinth (c. 405 BC) Won first prize as part of a trilogy with The Bacchae and Iphigenia in Aulis.

Lost and Fragmentary Plays (Not Dated)

Aegeus
Aeolus
Alcmene
Alope, or Cercyon
Antigone
Auge
Autolycus
Busiris
Cadmus
Chrysippus
Danae
Epeius
Eurystheus
Hippolytus Veiled
Ino
Ixion
Lamia
Licymnius
Meleager
Mysians
Oedipus
Oeneus
Oenomaus

www.ingramcontent.com/pod-product-compliance
Lightning Source LLC
Chambersburg PA
CBHW060100050426
42448CB00011B/2546